You're An Ace, Snoopy!

**Selected Cartoons from
THE WAY OF THE FUSSBUDGET
IS NOT EASY, Vol. I**

Charles M. Schulz

**CORONET BOOKS
Hodder and Stoughton**

PEANUTS comic strips by
Charles M. Schulz
Copyright © 1983, 1984 by United
Feature Syndicate, Inc.

First published in the United States of
America 1987 by Ballantine Books

Coronet edition 1988

This book comprises of a portion of
THE WAY OF THE FUSSBUDGET IS
NOT EASY and is reprinted by
arrangement with henry Holt and
Company Inc.

British Library C.I.P.

Schulz, Charles M.
    You're an ace, Snoopy! : selected
cartoons from The way of the fuss
budget is not easy, vol. 1.
I. Title
741.5'973   PN6728.P4

ISBN 0 340 42575 X

Printed and bound in Great Britain
for Hodder and Stoughton
Paperbacks, a division of Hodder and
Stoughton Ltd., Mill Road,
Dunton Green, Sevenoaks, Kent
TN13 2YA.
(Editorial Office: 47 Bedford Square,
London WC1B 3DP) by
Cox & Wyman Ltd., Reading.

You're an Ace, SNOOPY!

Dear Sweetheart,
Without you my
days are endless.

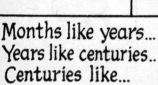

Days seem like
weeks...weeks like
months...

Months like years...
Years like centuries..
Centuries like...

You get the idea.

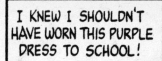

MADAM ABSOLUTELY, THERE IS NO DOUBT, FULLCHARGE

GET UP!

YOU'RE LYING IN MY BEANBAG

IT'S NOT YOUR BEANBAG, AND I WAS HERE FIRST...

LET'S MAKE AN AGREEMENT..

A WHAT?

Dear Linda,
Please send me an autographed photo of yourself.

Please sign it, "To my cute friend"

You may not believe this, but

I'm the cutest thing around here.

SCHULZ

NO, MA'AM, MY REPORT ISN'T READY...IT FELL OUT OF MY BINDER...

THE RINGS WOULDN'T CLOSE SO I TOOK IT BACK TO THE DEALER...

HE SAID THE RINGS NEEDED TO BE REPLACED, AND HE'D HAVE TO WRITE TO THE MANUFACTURER AND IT WOULD TAKE TWO WEEKS TO GET SPARE PARTS...

GOOD GOING, SIR...THAT WAS THE BEST EXCUSE I'VE EVER HEARD!

ANOTHER "D MINUS"! AM I GOING TO BE A "D MINUS" PERSON ALL MY LIFE, MARCIE? WHAT CAN I DO?

STAY AWAKE IN CLASS, STUDY HARD AND ALWAYS DO YOUR HOMEWORK

MAYBE I CAN THINK OF SOMETHING ELSE...

YES, MA'AM

THE ANSWER IS "NINE"

FEEL PRETTY SMUG, DON'T YOU, SIR?

AS SMUG AS A BUG IN A RUG!

HERE'S THE WORLD WAR I FLYING ACE SITTING IN A SMALL FRENCH CAFÉ...

HE IS VERY NERVOUS FROM HIS MANY DAYS AT THE FRONT...

HE NEEDS SOMETHING TO CALM HIS NERVES...

DECAFFEINATED ROOT BEER, S'IL VOUS PLAIT!

HERE'S THE WORLD WAR I FLYING ACE FLIRTING WITH THE BEAUTIFUL FRENCH WAITRESS...

I'LL TELL HER THE JOKE ABOUT THE TEN NURSES, THE FOUR PILOTS, THE BARBED WIRE AND THE CASE OF ROOT BEER...

I CAN NEVER REMEMBER HOW IT GOES...

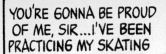

WHEN YOU LIVE ALONE IN THE DESERT, YOU HAVE TO MAKE UP YOUR OWN GAMES

I'LL BE THE QUARTERBACK AND YOU'LL BE THE RECEIVER...

HERE WE GO!

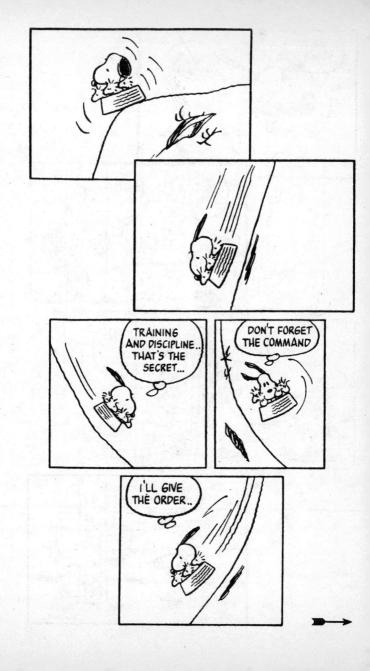

LOOK, MARCIE, I GOT A FORTUNE COOKIE IN MY LUNCH...

IT SAYS, "YOU ARE GOING TO GET AN IMPORTANT LETTER"

IT WAS RIGHT... I GOT AN IMPORTANT LETTER THIS MORNING...

A "D MINUS"!

WHEN YOU LIVE ALONE IN THE DESERT, YOU HAVE TO MAKE YOUR OWN PLEASURES...

GARÇON..

A MENU, PLEASE

Dear Spike,
How have you been?

Write when you have time.
Your brother,
Snoopy

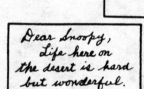

Dear Snoopy,
Life here on the desert is hard but wonderful.

Sometimes it is very hot

And the nights can be very cold.

➤➤

Sometimes we have rain and sudden flash floods.

Sometimes it even snows.

But there are always beautiful places to walk and things to see.

And when I return home...

I always have a place to hang my hat.

YES, MA'AM, I ENJOYED THE CONCERT VERY MUCH.. I'M INTO CLASSICAL MUSIC

OF COURSE, SOME UNCULTURED TYPES TEND TO FALL ASLEEP, BUT WHAT CAN YOU EXPECT?

BLEAH!!

GIVE HER A "D MINUS," MA'AM...WHIP HER INTO SHAPE!

IT WAS A "YOUNG PEOPLE'S CONCERT," CHUCK...YOU KNOW, GET THE KIDS ACQUAINTED WITH GOOD MUSIC...

ANYWAY, AT FIRST I DIDN'T EVEN WANT TO GO, BUT AFTER I HEARD THE MUSIC, I THOUGHT IT WAS GREAT...

SO NOW WHAT HAPPENS? NOW WE HAVE TO WRITE A FIVE-HUNDRED WORD THEME ON THE CONCERT

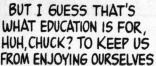

BUT I GUESS THAT'S WHAT EDUCATION IS FOR, HUH, CHUCK? TO KEEP US FROM ENJOYING OURSELVES

WHAT WOULD YOU DO IF I KICKED THAT OVER?

PROBABLY NOTHING AT THE MOMENT...

BUT YEARS FROM NOW, AFTER YOU'RE MARRIED AND YOU AND YOUR HUSBAND WANT ME TO CO-SIGN A NOTE SO YOU CAN BUY A NEW HOUSE, I'LL REFUSE!

YOUNGER BROTHERS LEARN TO THINK FAST

TEARS... LIKE IN "CRYING."

SCIENTISTS ARE NOW STUDYING TEARS, DID YOU KNOW THAT?

THEY'LL PROBABLY WANT TO MAKE A SPECIAL STUDY OF BEAGLE TEARS...

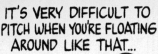

MATURITY IS WHAT YOU SHOULD STRIVE FOR, CHARLIE BROWN...

THE DOCTOR IS IN

A MATURE PERSON IS A PATIENT PERSON... SOMEBODY WHO DOESN'T DEMAND EVERYTHING **NOW**!

THE DOCTOR

THAT'S GOOD TO KNOW BECAUSE I CAN'T PAY YOU UNTIL TOMORROW...

TOMORROW?! ARE YOU OUT OF YOUR MIND?!!

HERE'S THE WORLD WAR I FLYING ACE FLIRTING WITH THE BEAUTIFUL FRENCH WAITRESS...

HI, SWEETIE..

DID YOU KNOW THAT THE FOAM ON ROOT BEER COMES FROM THE SAP OF THE DESERT YUCCA TREE?

I THINK I NEED A BETTER OPENING LINE...

Dear Brother Snoopy,
Life here on the
desert is good.

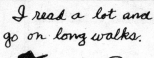

I read a lot and
go on long walks.

When there is nothing
else to do, I practice
a few field goals.

BY THE TIME I'VE GROWN UP, WE'LL PROBABLY HAVE A WOMAN PRESIDENT..

YOU KNOW WHAT THAT MEANS, DON'T YOU?

IT MEANS I WON'T GET TO BE THE FIRST ONE...

BOY, THAT MAKES ME MAD!!

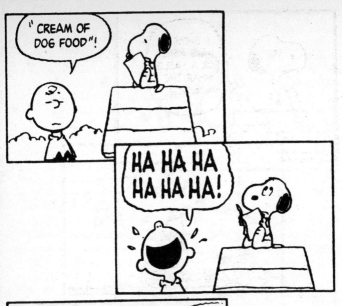

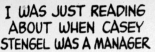

I WAS JUST READING ABOUT WHEN CASEY STENGEL WAS A MANAGER

HE ONCE TIPPED HIS CAP TO AN UMPIRE AND A BIRD FLEW OUT!

THAT MUST HAVE BEEN FUNNY..I WISH I HAD SEEN THAT...

YIPE!

WELL, MA'AM, MY MATH PAPER IS SOMEWHERE ALONG THIRD STREET, MY ENGLISH THEME WAS LAST SEEN ON SELBY AVENUE AND MY HISTORY PAPER IS NOW FLYING OVER HIGHLAND PARK...

TURN OUT THE LIGHTS, MA'AM, AND LET'S GO HOME!

WHEN YOU'RE DEPRESSED, IT ALWAYS HELPS TO LEAN YOUR HEAD ON YOUR ARM

ARMS LIKE TO FEEL USEFUL

I'M GLAD YOU'RE NOT LIKE SOME BASEBALL MANAGERS, CHARLIE BROWN

I READ ABOUT ONE MANAGER WHO USED TO GET REAL MAD AT HIS PLAYERS...

IF A PLAYER DID SOMETHING DUMB, THE MANAGER WOULD PULL THE PLAYER'S CAP DOWN OVER HIS HEAD..

I SHOULDN'T HAVE MENTIONED IT...

SCHULZ

STRIKE THREE!

THAT'S FOR SWINGING AT A PITCH THAT WAS SIX FEET OVER YOUR HEAD!

WHAT DID YOU OTHER GUYS DO WRONG?

I MISSED AN EASY FLY BALL

ME TOO

I SLEPT THROUGH THE THIRD INNING

So I bundled up my drawings and set off for Hollywood.

I had a new idea that I was sure they couldn't resist.

NEEDLES ←   HOLLYWOOD →

I went into the first studio I could find and offered them my great idea for a new movie.

ACE
Productions

NO, WE'RE SORRY, BUT WE DON'T THINK IT WOULD BE A GOOD IDEA TO ANIMATE "CITIZEN KANE"

RATS!

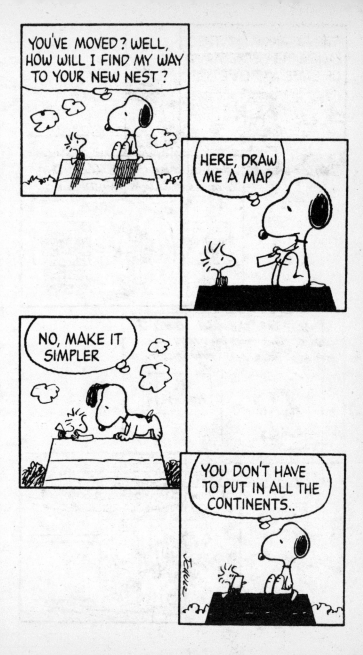

THE ATLANTIC AND THE PACIFIC, THE SECRETARY OF STATE AND CAPE COD...

THE DARK AGES, THE GULF OF MEXICO, NOVA SCOTIA, NEW YORK...

PING!

THAT'S IT, MA'AM... MY HEAD IS FULL!!

MMM! THERE'S NOTHING THAT SMELLS AS GOOD AS PASTE!

YES, MA'AM, I JUST LOVE THE SMELL OF THIS WHITE PASTE...

YOU SHOULD PUT A LITTLE BEHIND EACH EAR TONIGHT WHEN YOU GO OUT WITH YOUR BOYFRIEND

JUST A LITTLE ROMANTIC SUGGESTION...

WATCH THIS, MARCIE... TEACHERS ALWAYS GIVE GOOD GRADES TO GIRLS WHO HAVE RIBBONS IN THEIR HAIR...

NO, MA'AM, I DON'T KNOW THE ANSWER, BUT I HAVE RIBBONS IN MY HAIR...

THE ANSWER WAS "TWELVE," SIR

EVEN IF YOU HAVE RIBBONS IN YOUR HAIR, TEACHERS DON'T LIKE YOU IF YOU HAVE A BIG NOSE..

YES, MA'AM, I WALKED TO SCHOOL IN THE RAIN..I HAD TO PUT MY BINDER ON MY HEAD TO KEEP FROM GETTING SOAKED...

MY REPORT? WELL, IT'S INSIDE THE BINDER, AND I THINK THE BINDER HAS RUSTED TO MY HEAD...